Georgia, My State
Geographic Regions

Lower Coastal Plain

by Doraine Bennett

STATE STANDARDS PUBLISHING

Your State • Your Standards • Your Grade Level

Dear Educators, Librarians and Parents . . .

Thank you for choosing the *"Georgia, My State"* Series! We have designed this series to support the Georgia Department of Education's Georgia Performance Standards for elementary level Georgia studies. Each book in the series has been written at appropriate grade level as measured by the ATOS Readability Formula for Books (Accelerated Reader), the Lexile Framework for Reading, and the Fountas & Pinnell Benchmark Assessment System for Guided Reading. Photographs and/or illustrations, captions, and other design elements have been included to provide supportive visual messaging to enhance text comprehension. Glossary and Word Index sections introduce key new words and help young readers develop skills in locating and combining information.

We wish you all success in using the *"Georgia, My State"* Series to meet your student or child's learning needs. For additional sources of information, see www.georgiaencyclopedia.org.

Jill Ward, President

Publisher
State Standards Publishing, LLC
1788 Quail Hollow
Hamilton, GA 31811
USA
1.866.740.3056
www.statestandardspublishing.com

Library of Congress Cataloging-in-Publication Data
Bennett, Doraine, 1953-
  Lower Coastal Plain / by Doraine Bennett.
      p. cm. -- (Georgia, my state. Geographic Regions)
  Includes index.
  ISBN-13: 978-1-935077-49-7 (hardcover)
  ISBN-10: 1-935077-49-X (hardcover)
  ISBN-13: 978-1-935077-50-3 (pbk.)
  ISBN-10: 1-935077-50-3 (pbk.)
  1. Georgia--Juvenile literature. 2. Georgia--Geography--Juvenile literature. I. Title.
  F286.3.B4658 2009
  917.58'7--dc22
                                                2009013003

Table of Contents

The land is very flat here. Some of it is covered in water.

Appalachian Plateau

Blue Ridge

Valley and Ridge

Piedmont

Upper Coastal Plain

Lower Coastal Plain

Atlantic Ocean

The Lower Coastal Plain is near the Atlantic Ocean.

Land Near the Ocean

Hi, I'm Bagster! Let's explore the Lower Coastal Plain **geographic region**. A region is an area named for the way the land is formed. The lower part of this region is near the **Atlantic Ocean**. The land is very flat here. Some of the land is covered in water.

Most of Georgia's beaches are on the Barrier Islands.

Barrier Islands

Atlantic Ocean

Barrier Islands protect the mainland from the waves and wind.

Let's Go to the Beach

Land at the ocean is called a **coast**. A chain of islands stretches along the Georgia coast. They are called the **Barrier Islands**. They protect the mainland of Georgia. They block the ocean waves and wind. Most of Georgia's beaches are on these islands. Let's build a sand castle!

A boat from the ocean is coming into this estuary.

A marsh is land that is covered in shallow water.

Georgia's Coast Changes

Georgia's coast is not all beaches. Some parts are **marshes**. A marsh is a place where shallow water covers the land. Grasses grow here. Some parts of the coast are **estuaries**. An estuary is a place where fresh water from a river meets salt water from the ocean.

Deer live on
the islands.

Wild horses run
free on
Cumberland
Island!

We must take a boat to some of the Barrier Islands.

Wild Horses Live on the Island!

There are no bridges to some of the Barrier Islands. We must take a boat. Scientists study animals and plants on **Cumberland Island**. Live oak trees grow there. Deer live there. Wild horses live on the island, too. Be careful! They don't like people.

Coast

Continental
Shelf

Slope

Ocean
Floor

MY STATE

The ocean is not very deep near the coast.

How Deep is the Ocean?

The ocean is not very deep near the Georgia coast. The ocean bottom slants like a swimming pool. This piece of the ocean floor is called the **continental shelf**. It would look like a shelf if you could see it.

Tomochichi and Mary Musgrove helped James Oglethorpe start Savannah.

Savannah was the first city in Georgia.

This is what Savannah looks like today.

People You Know Lived Here

Creek Indians once lived in the Lower Coastal Plain. Tomochichi and Mary Musgrove were Creek Indians. They helped James Oglethorpe start **Savannah**. It was the first city in Georgia.

Large ships sail up the Savannah River!

Many ships carry boxes filled with things people buy and sell.

Tugboats help move big ships into the harbor.

Let's Sail into Savannah!

Savannah is an important **port**. Large ships bring things here. They sail up the **Savannah River**. They carry huge boxes to the **harbor**. A harbor is a safe place for boats to land. The boxes are full of things people buy and sell. Tugboats pull big ships into the harbor. Let's catch a ride!

Watch out for alligators!

Appalachian Plateau

Blue Ridge

Valley and Ridge

Piedmont

Upper Coastal Plain

Lower Coastal Plain

Okefenokee Swamp

Atlantic Ocean

Let's paddle a canoe in the Okefenokee Swamp.

Watch Out for Alligators!

Let's paddle a canoe in the **Okefenokee Swamp**. The name means *trembling earth*. Floating islands rest on tree roots or dead plants under the dark water. The ground trembles and shakes when you step on it. It's scary! Alligators live in the Okefenokee Swamp. Watch out!

Pitcher plants eat insects!

This spider might fall in!

These Plants Eat Insects!

Pitcher plants grow in the **swamp**.

They hold water in their leaves.

Insects sometimes fall into the leaf.

Stiff hairs at the top won't let them

crawl out again. The

leaf **digests** the bugs!

It eats them for food!

Glossary

Atlantic Ocean – The ocean that Georgia has its coast on.

Barrier Islands – A chain of islands that protect the mainland of Georgia from the wind and waves of the ocean.

coast – The place where land meets the ocean.

continental shelf – The shallow ocean floor near the coast.

Cumberland Island – One of Georgia's Barrier Islands. Wild horses live there.

digest – To eat something and use it as food.

estuary – A place where fresh water from a river meets salt water from the ocean.

geographic region – An area named for the way the land is formed.

harbor – A safe place for boats to land.

marsh – A place where shallow water and grasses cover the land.

Okefenokee Swamp – The largest swamp in Georgia. It is one of the largest swamps in the United States.

port – A place where large ships bring things.

Savannah – The first city in Georgia.

Savannah River – The large river at the port of Savannah.

swamp – A place where fresh water and floating islands cover the land.

Word Index

Image Credits

About the Author

Doraine Bennett has a degree in professional writing from Columbus State University in Columbus, Georgia, and has been writing and teaching writing for over twenty years. She has authored numerous articles in magazines for both children and adults and is the editor of the National Infantry Association's *Infantry Bugler* magazine. Doraine enjoys reading and writing books and articles for children. She lives in Georgia with her husband, Cliff.